HRH Prince John Charles Wright

HRH Prince Joe Duncan Wright

Advances in semiconductor technologies

1st Published in 1999

2nd Publication in 2008

Table of Contents

Introduction

Advances in semiconductor technologies have been rapid and transformative, shaping the modern world in numerous ways. Advancements in semiconductor technologies have significantly influenced various sectors and revolutionised the modern world Semiconductors are at the heart of computing devices. Advancements in semiconductor technology have led to the development of faster, smaller, and more powerful microprocessors. Moore's Law, which predicted the doubling of transistors on a chip every two years, has largely held true and has enabled continuous improvements in computing power. The miniaturisation and increased efficiency of semiconductors have made portable devices like smartphones and tablets powerful and energy-efficient. This has led to a revolution in communication, entertainment, and productivity, changing the way we interact and access information.

Semiconductor advancements have played a crucial role in the growth of the IoT. Smaller, more energy-efficient chips have allowed for the connection of various devices, enabling the seamless exchange of data and automation in various industries. Artificial intelligence heavily relies on high-performance computing. Advanced semiconductors, particularly Graphics

Processing Units (GPUs) and specialized AI chips (like TPUs), have significantly enhanced the capabilities of AI by enabling faster processing and more complex computation. Semiconductors are crucial in medical devices and equipment. They have facilitated the development of more precise imaging tools, wearable health trackers, and advancements in personalized medicine, improving diagnosis, treatment, and patient care.

Semiconductor technology has contributed to the growth of renewable energy sources, particularly in solar panels. Advances in photovoltaic cells, which convert sunlight into electricity, have increased efficiency and decreased costs, making solar power more accessible. Semiconductors have transformed vehicles by enabling advanced safety features, infotainment systems, and the development of electric and autonomous vehicles. The automotive industry heavily relies on semiconductor technology for sensors, control units, and communication systems.

Semiconductor-based sensors and devices are used for environmental monitoring, enabling more accurate and efficient data collection for climate, air, and water quality assessments. Semiconductors play a critical role in cybersecurity. Advanced chips help in developing more secure systems, enabling encryption, secure communication, and protection against cyber threats. Semiconductor technology is integral in the advancement of smart manufacturing, automation, and robotics.

These technologies have improved efficiency, precision, and output in various industries.

Miniaturisation

Moore's Law, the observation that the number of transistors on a microchip doubles about every two years, has driven the Miniaturisation of transistors. This has led to more powerful and energy-efficient chips. Advances in Miniaturisation have been at the forefront of semiconductor technologies, driving the evolution of electronic devices to become smaller, faster, and more powerful. This trend is primarily attributed to Moore's Law, which predicted that the number of transistors on a microchip would double approximately every two years, leading to a consistent reduction in the size of individual transistors.

Transistor Scaling

Miniaturisation involves shrinking the size of transistors, the fundamental building blocks of digital devices. As transistors get smaller, more can be packed onto a single chip, leading to increased computational power. Transistor scaling is a critical aspect of the Miniaturisation process in semiconductor technology. It refers to the practice of reducing the size of individual transistors, which are the fundamental building blocks of electronic circuits. Transistor scaling has been a driving force behind the advancement of computing and electronic devices, enabling them to become smaller, faster, and more energy-efficient. Let's take a closer look at the significance and implications of transistor scaling in the context of semiconductor miniaturization.

Transistor scaling involves making transistors smaller by reducing their dimensions, such as the width and length of the transistor's gate. As transistors shrink, more of them can fit onto a single semiconductor chip. The ability to fit more transistors on a chip leads to higher integration density. This enables the integration of multiple functions and components on a single chip, such as logic gates, memory cells, and other functionalities.

Smaller transistors can switch on and off more quickly due to shorter distances for charge carriers to travel. This results in improved processing speeds and overall device performance. Smaller transistors require less power to operate, leading to lower energy consumption and improved energy efficiency. This is crucial for extending battery life in portable devices.

Miniaturized transistors generate less heat due to their reduced size and power consumption. This makes it easier to manage heat dissipation within the device, improving reliability. As the size of transistors decreases, more chips can be produced from a single silicon wafer. This economies of scale lead to cost reductions in manufacturing.

Transistor scaling faces challenges as transistors approach atomic dimensions. Quantum effects, leakage currents, and thermal issues become more prominent at these scales, necessitating innovative solutions in materials and design. Achieving smaller transistor sizes requires advancements in photolithography, the process used to create intricate patterns on semiconductor wafers. Advanced lithography techniques enable finer features to be etched onto the wafer. Transistor scaling cannot continue indefinitely due to the laws of physics. As transistors approach atomic sizes, quantum effects start to dominate, and the control of charge carriers becomes more challenging.

Beyond Moore's Law

Transistor scaling has been a driving force behind Moore's Law, which predicted the doubling of transistor count every two years. As we approach the physical limits of scaling, new technologies like three-dimensional (3D) transistors and alternative materials are explored to extend the benefits of miniaturization. The concept that the traditional trends of Moore's Law, which predicts the doubling of the number of transistors on a semiconductor chip approximately every two years, may not be sustainable in the long term due to physical and technological limitations. Moore's Law has driven the rapid advancement of computing and technology for decades, leading to the Miniaturisation and increased performance of electronic devices. However, as transistors become smaller and approach atomic scales, challenges arise that could hinder the continuation of this exponential growth. The concept of "Beyond Moore's Law" acknowledges that the traditional approach of shrinking transistors to improve performance and efficiency may encounter obstacles.

As transistors approach atomic sizes, quantum effects become more pronounced, leading to challenges in controlling charge carriers and maintaining reliable operation. Leakage currents and heat dissipation also become significant concerns. The intricate process of manufacturing increasingly smaller transistors becomes more complex and costly. The precision required for lithography and other fabrication techniques becomes harder to achieve.

The economics of manufacturing may become less favourable as the cost of developing and producing ever-smaller transistors increases, potentially leading to diminishing returns. While smaller transistors are more power-efficient in some cases, further Miniaturisation can lead to power leakage and other inefficiencies that counteract the energy savings.

To address these challenges and continue advancing technology, researchers and the industry are exploring alternative strategies and technologies "beyond Moore's Law." Some of these approaches are included here. Stacking multiple layers of transistors can increase density and performance without relying solely on shrinking transistor sizes. Exploring alternative materials with unique electronic properties that can replace or supplement traditional silicon in transistors. Leveraging the principles of quantum mechanics to develop computing models that can solve complex problems beyond the capabilities of classical computers.

Designing computers inspired by the human brain's architecture to achieve high efficiency and processing power for certain tasks. Using light instead of traditional electrical signals to perform computations, enabling faster processing and data transfer.

Exploring new computing paradigms that go beyond the traditional von Neumann architecture to optimize performance and energy efficiency.

Developing application-specific hardware optimized for specific tasks, such as artificial intelligence and machine learning. The shift "beyond Moore's Law" signifies a transition from relying solely on transistor scaling to a more holistic approach that combines various technological innovations. While the pace of advancement may change, the drive to continue improving computing power, efficiency, and capabilities remains strong. Researchers, engineers, and technologists are working together to explore new avenues and ensure that the trajectory of technological progress continues well into the future.

Increased Performance

Smaller transistors allow for faster switching speeds and reduced signal propagation distances. This results in improved processing speed and overall device performance. Increased performance through Miniaturisation is a key driver in semiconductor technologies. Miniaturisation refers to the process of shrinking the size of electronic components, particularly transistors, on semiconductor chips. This trend has enabled the development of smaller, faster, and more energy-efficient devices, leading to significant advancements in various industries.

As transistors and other components are scaled down, more of them can be packed onto a single chip. This higher density leads to greater processing power and improved overall performance. Miniaturisation allows electrons to travel shorter distances within transistors, reducing the time it takes for signals to pass through. This results in faster processing speeds and quicker data transfer rates.

Smaller transistors require less energy to switch on and off, leading to lower power consumption. This has important implications for extending battery life in portable devices and reducing energy costs in data centres.

Miniaturization reduces the distance between components, which improves heat dissipation. This helps prevent overheating and allows devices to operate at higher speeds without becoming too hot. Miniaturisation enables the integration of more functionalities onto a single chip. This integration can include multiple processing units, memory, graphics, and other specialized functions, all in a compact form factor.

Smaller transistors and shorter signal paths result in reduced latency, which is critical for applications requiring real-time processing, such as gaming and high-frequency trading. As Miniaturisation continues, manufacturing techniques must become more precise and sophisticated. This drives the development of innovative fabrication methods and technologies. Miniaturisation has paved the way for nanoscale technologies, which explore the unique properties of materials at extremely small scales. This has led to innovations in areas like quantum computing and nanoelectronics. Miniaturisation has played a pivotal role in the advancement of high-performance computing systems. Supercomputers, which require immense processing power, have benefited from the ability to pack more processing units into a smaller space.

Miniaturization has enabled the creation of smaller and more energy-efficient sensors and components, driving the growth of the Internet of Things (IoT) and wearable technology markets. It's important to note that while Miniaturisation has delivered remarkable performance improvements, it also presents challenges. Quantum effects, power leakage, and the limitations of traditional manufacturing processes can impact performance gains at extremely small scales. As a result, researchers are exploring alternative materials, fabrication techniques, and computing paradigms to continue pushing the boundaries of performance beyond what traditional Miniaturisation can achieve. Increased performance through Miniaturisation has been a driving force in the evolution of electronics, enabling devices to become faster, more capable, and more accessible to a wide range of applications and users.

Higher Density

More transistors can be placed on a single chip, leading to higher device density. This is particularly significant for memory chips, as it allows for greater data storage capacity. Higher density is a crucial aspect of Miniaturisation in semiconductor technologies, and it refers to the ability to fit more transistors and electronic components onto a single chip. This density increase has played a pivotal role in advancing the capabilities of electronic devices, from microprocessors and memory chips to sensors and integrated circuits. Let's how higher density is achieved and its significance.

The primary method to achieve higher density is by scaling down the size of transistors and other components. As transistors become smaller, more of them can be packed into the same physical space on a chip. Advanced lithography techniques, such as extreme ultraviolet (EUV) lithography, enable the printing of finer features on semiconductor wafers. This allows for the creation of smaller transistors and interconnects, leading to higher density. Instead of only scaling down in two dimensions, 3D integration involves stacking transistors and components on top of each other. This approach increases the effective density of a chip and enhances performance. The use of new materials with superior electrical properties can allow for the creation of smaller transistors without compromising performance.

Higher density enables the integration of more transistors, which in turn allows for more complex and powerful microprocessors. This leads to improved computational capabilities and faster data processing. The increased density also allows for larger and denser memory chips, leading to greater storage capacity in devices like smartphones, laptops, and servers. Higher density enables the creation of smaller devices that can perform tasks that previously required larger equipment. This has led to the development of compact yet powerful smartphones, tablets, and wearable devices. As transistors become smaller and more densely packed, they require less energy to operate. This leads to improved energy efficiency and longer battery life in portable devices.

Higher density has paved the way for emerging technologies such as artificial intelligence (AI), machine learning, and edge computing. These technologies demand significant processing power and memory, which higher density can provide. In data centres, higher density chips enable the packing of more computing power in a smaller space, optimizing data processing and reducing energy consumption. The Internet of Things (IoT) relies on compact yet capable devices with integrated sensors. Higher density allows for the creation of such devices, facilitating IoT growth.

Higher density in semiconductors has opened doors to scientific research and simulations that were previously impractical due to computing limitations. Higher density often leads to cost savings, as manufacturers can produce more chips from a single wafer, reducing production costs per unit. The pursuit of higher density drives continuous innovation in semiconductor manufacturing and materials science, pushing the boundaries of what's possible in electronics. Achieving higher density through Miniaturisation is a fundamental principle in semiconductor technologies. It has reshaped industries, transformed the way we use technology, and contributed to the rapid advancement of various fields, from computing to communication to healthcare.

Reduced Power Consumption

Smaller transistors require less power to operate. As a result, devices with miniaturized components are more energy-efficient, leading to longer battery life in portable devices. Reduced power consumption is a significant outcome of the ongoing Miniaturisation in semiconductor technologies. As electronic components become smaller and more densely packed on a chip, they inherently require less power to operate. This achievement has far-reaching implications for various industries and applications, leading to more energy-efficient devices and systems. Let's look how reduced power consumption is achieved and its broader impact.

As transistors are scaled down, they become more energy-efficient. Smaller transistors require lower voltages to switch on and off, resulting in reduced power consumption. Smaller transistors experience less leakage current, where electricity flows through even when a transistor is supposed to be off. This reduction in leakage contributes to lower overall power consumption. With miniaturization, the operating voltage of transistors can be scaled down. Lower operating voltages translate to reduced power requirements. Modern processors and chips can dynamically adjust their operating voltage and frequency based on workload. This enables energy savings during periods of lower processing demand. Chip designers implement sophisticated power management techniques to optimize power consumption based on usage patterns.

Let's look at the broader Impact of Reduced Power Consumption. In portable devices such as smartphones, laptops, and wearables, reduced power consumption translates to longer battery life. Users can go longer between charges, enhancing convenience. Reduced power consumption is essential for energy-efficient computing, particularly in data centres and server farms. It helps reduce the environmental impact of data processing. The reduced energy requirements contribute to green computing initiatives, which aim to minimize the carbon footprint of IT and electronics.

Lower power consumption results in less heat generation, reducing the need for elaborate cooling solutions. This has practical implications for device design and maintenance. Lower power consumption can lead to less stress on electronic components, potentially extending their lifespan and improving overall device reliability. IoT devices often operate on battery power or energy harvesting. Reduced power consumption enables the development of IoT devices that can run for extended periods on limited energy sources.

Wearable devices, such as fitness trackers and smartwatches, benefit from reduced power consumption as it allows for compact designs and prolonged usage between charges.

Reduced power consumption is crucial for embedded systems that need to operate reliably in remote or inaccessible locations. Energy-efficient semiconductor technology is crucial for medical devices that are implanted within the body or are designed to operate on battery power. In remote sensing applications, such as environmental monitoring or space exploration, reduced power consumption is critical for extending mission lifetimes. In aerospace and defence applications, where power constraints are common, reduced power consumption enables the development of efficient and long-lasting systems.

In summary, reduced power consumption due to Miniaturisation in semiconductor technologies has transformed the electronics landscape. It has ushered in an era of energy-efficient computing, enabling longer battery life, environmental sustainability, and innovation across various sectors. This trend is expected to continue as semiconductor manufacturers and researchers explore new ways to optimize power usage while advancing technology capabilities.

Improved Heat Dissipation

Smaller components generate less heat due to reduced power consumption. This makes it easier to manage heat dissipation within devices, leading to enhanced reliability. Improved heat dissipation is a critical aspect of Miniaturisation in semiconductor technologies. As electronic components become smaller and more densely packed on a chip, managing heat generated during operation becomes increasingly challenging. Effective heat dissipation is essential to prevent overheating, ensure optimal performance, and maintain the reliability and longevity of semiconductor devices. Let's take a look at how improved heat dissipation is achieved and its significance.

New materials with higher thermal conductivity are integrated into chip designs to enhance the transfer of heat away from critical components. Heat spreading techniques, such as using heat spreaders or heat pipes, are employed to evenly distribute heat across the chip surface and facilitate efficient dissipation. Chip designers optimize the microarchitecture to evenly distribute processing loads, preventing localized hotspots and reducing the overall heat generated. High-performance thermal interface materials are used between components to enhance heat transfer between different layers of the chip. In 3D-stacked chip designs, components are layered on top of each other, reducing the distance heat needs to travel and improving thermal efficiency. Some chips incorporate micro-scale cooling solutions, such as microfluidic channels or embedded micro fans, to actively dissipate heat.

Excessive heat can lead to component failure, reduced performance, and even permanent damage. Effective heat dissipation helps prevent such issues. Many semiconductor devices, including CPUs and GPUs, operate optimally within specific temperature ranges. Improved heat dissipation ensures that devices maintain their performance levels without thermal throttling. High temperatures can accelerate wear and tear on components. Effective heat management extends the lifespan and enhances the reliability of semiconductor devices.

Stable and controlled temperatures contribute to consistent performance over extended periods, which is especially important for devices that require continuous operation. Overheating can lead to increased power consumption and inefficiency. Improved heat dissipation helps maintain optimal power efficiency. Efficient heat management enables the development of compact, slim devices without compromising performance or safety. Some applications, such as automotive electronics or medical devices, require strict adherence to temperature limits for safety reasons.

In data centres, efficient heat dissipation reduces the need for excessive cooling, leading to energy savings and improved overall efficiency. As chips become smaller and more complex, thermal design becomes more challenging. Improved heat dissipation addresses these challenges. Devices that generate less heat are more comfortable for users to handle, especially in portable devices like laptops and smartphones. Energy-efficient heat dissipation contributes to reducing the environmental footprint of electronic devices, as less power is needed for cooling. Efficient heat management aligns with sustainability goals by ensuring longer device lifespans and reducing electronic waste.

In conclusion, improved heat dissipation is a crucial aspect of Miniaturisation in semiconductor technologies. It plays a pivotal role in ensuring the reliability, performance, and longevity of semiconductor devices, ranging from microprocessors to advanced electronic systems. As the demand for smaller, more powerful devices continues to grow, effective heat management remains a priority for semiconductor manufacturers and researchers.

Integration of Functionalities

Miniaturization enables the integration of multiple functions on a single chip. This integration leads to complex systems-on-chip (SoCs) that combine processing, memory, and other functionalities. Integration of functionalities is a key aspect of Miniaturisation in semiconductor technologies, aimed at packing more capabilities into smaller and more efficient chips. This approach involves combining multiple functions and components onto a single semiconductor device or chip, resulting in enhanced performance, reduced power consumption, and overall improved efficiency. Let's look at the overview of the integration of functionalities and its significance.

SoC is a prime example of integration, where various components like processors, memory, sensors, and communication interfaces are integrated onto a single chip. This reduces the need for separate components, minimizes interconnects, and enhances communication between functions. Combining analogue and digital functionalities on a single chip is crucial for applications like IoT devices, where sensors and communication circuits coexist with processing units.

Sensors, such as accelerometers, gyroscopes, and environmental sensors, are often integrated into chips to enable diverse applications, from smartphones to wearable devices. Combining memory elements like RAM, ROM, and flash memory onto a chip enhances data access speed and reduces power consumption. Integrating wireless communication interfaces (e.g., Wi-Fi, Bluetooth, 5G) into chips allows for seamless connectivity in devices. Integrated digital-to-analogue (DAC) and analogue-to-digital (ADC) converters enable processing and conversion of signals within a single chip. On-chip power management functions, such as voltage regulators, optimize power consumption and enhance efficiency.

Integrating multiple functions onto a single chip reduces the need for separate components, leading to smaller devices with compact form factors. Integration reduces interconnect length, which minimizes signal loss and power consumption. It also enables power management features for improved efficiency. Fewer components and simpler assembly lead to reduced manufacturing costs. Integration reduces signal delays and enhances data exchange between functions, resulting in improved overall performance. Fewer interconnects mean fewer potential points of failure, contributing to increased device reliability. Integration reduces the length of signal traces, minimizing electromagnetic interference and enhancing signal integrity. Integrating functionalities frees up physical space, allowing for the addition of other features or components.

Integrated chips can be designed to cater to specific application requirements, allowing for tailored solutions. Fewer components and interconnects streamline assembly processes, reducing complexities and potential errors. Integrated designs can be scaled easily by adding more instances of the integrated functionalities. Integrated functionalities result in devices with smoother, more seamless operations and improved user experiences. Integration supports the development of advanced applications that require multiple functions to work harmoniously.

Compact devices are desirable for various applications, including wearable technology, IoT, and mobile devices. Integrating functionalities anticipates future technological requirements and helps devices remain relevant over time. In conclusion, the integration of functionalities in miniaturisation within semiconductor technologies has revolutionized the electronics industry. It has paved the way for smaller, more efficient, and feature-rich devices that cater to various applications. As technology continues to advance, the trend of integration is expected to play a crucial role in shaping the future of semiconductor design and innovation.

Mobile and Wearable Devices

The Miniaturisation of components has played a crucial role in the development of smartphones, tablets, and wearable devices. These devices are compact yet capable of performing a wide range of tasks. The Miniaturisation of semiconductor technologies has played a pivotal role in shaping the landscape of mobile and wearable devices. From smartphones and smartwatches to fitness trackers and augmented reality glasses, Miniaturisation has enabled these devices to become increasingly compact, efficient, and powerful. Here's how Miniaturisation has impacted the realm of mobile and wearable devices:

Miniaturization has allowed mobile devices like smartphones to become sleek and lightweight, making them more portable and convenient for users to carry around. Despite their compact sizes, miniaturized semiconductor components have facilitated the integration of powerful processors, memory, and other functionalities, resulting in high-performance mobile and wearable devices.

Smaller components consume less power, contributing to improved energy efficiency and longer battery life in mobile devices and wearables. Miniaturized sensors, such as accelerometers, gyroscopes, and heart rate monitors, have enabled the development of innovative wearable devices that can track fitness, monitor health, and even enable virtual reality experiences.

Wearables equipped with miniaturized semiconductor components can collect and process real-time data, providing users with immediate feedback and insights into their activities. Miniaturisation has allowed the integration of multiple functions into a single device, such as combining communication, health monitoring, and entertainment features in smartwatches.

Miniaturized chips support wireless communication technologies like Bluetooth, Wi-Fi, and cellular connectivity, enabling seamless communication and data transfer between devices and networks. Wearable devices are designed to comfortably fit on the body, and miniaturized components have made it possible to create devices with ergonomic and unobtrusive designs. Miniaturized components have facilitated the creation of wearable devices that cater to individuals with disabilities, enhancing accessibility and inclusivity. The small size of semiconductor components allows for greater customization and personalization of wearable devices to suit individual preferences and needs.

Miniaturization has enabled the creation of AR and VR wearable devices that can provide immersive experiences, whether for entertainment, training, or professional applications. As

Miniaturisation continues to advance, the potential for even smaller and more sophisticated mobile and wearable devices becomes more promising, leading to innovations we might not even envision yet. Miniaturized components are essential for IoT devices, which often need to be compact and energy-efficient while maintaining connectivity and functionality. Miniaturized semiconductor technologies enable the development of wearables that monitor vital signs, detect irregularities, and provide insights into users' health and wellness.

In summary, Miniaturisation in semiconductor technologies has transformed the landscape of mobile and wearable devices. It has empowered the creation of devices that are smaller, more powerful, and capable of performing a wide range of functions. As the technology continues to evolve, we can expect mobile and wearable devices to become even more integrated, efficient, and seamlessly integrated into our daily lives.

Space Efficiency

Miniaturisation allows for devices to become more compact and lightweight. This is particularly important for applications where space is limited, such as in medical implants and aerospace technologies. Space efficiency is a crucial aspect of Miniaturisation in semiconductor technologies. It refers to the ability to pack more transistors, components, and functionalities into a smaller physical space on a semiconductor chip. This concept has revolutionized the electronics industry, enabling the creation of smaller, more powerful, and versatile devices. Let's look at how space efficiency plays a pivotal role in miniaturization.

Space-efficient semiconductor designs allow for a higher level of integration on a single chip. This means that more components, such as transistors, resistors, and capacitors, can be packed into a limited space, leading to greater functionality. As components become smaller and more densely packed, the overall footprint of electronic devices decreases. This is particularly important for mobile devices and wearables where compactness is essential. Smaller components often require less power to operate, contributing to energy efficiency. Moreover, optimizing the space usage on a chip reduces the distances that signals need to travel, leading to lower power consumption.

Space-efficient designs allow for the integration of more complex circuits and advanced functionalities. This leads to improved device performance, speed, and capabilities. With space-efficient designs, it becomes feasible to include multiple functionalities on a single chip. This is particularly advantageous for devices that require various sensors, communication modules, and processing units.

Space efficiency has driven the development of innovative packaging techniques, such as System-on-Chip (SoC) and System-in-Package (SiP), which further enhance integration and compactness. Sensors, such as accelerometers, gyroscopes, and environmental sensors, can be miniaturized and integrated onto chips, enabling devices to gather data more accurately and efficiently.

Space-efficient semiconductor designs enable the integration of wireless communication modules, such as Bluetooth and Wi-Fi, allowing devices to communicate seamlessly with other devices and networks. The Internet of Things (IoT) relies on space-efficient semiconductor technologies to create small, energy-efficient devices that can be embedded in various objects to gather and transmit data.

Space efficiency is critical in the development of wearables, as these devices need to be compact, lightweight, and comfortable to wear while maintaining high performance and functionality.

Space-efficient semiconductor designs have paved the way for the development of miniaturized medical devices that can be implanted in the body for monitoring and treatment purposes. Space-efficient chips are crucial for powering the sensors and processors in robots and automated systems, enabling precise and efficient operation.

In essence, space efficiency in Miniaturisation drives the creation of smaller, more powerful, and feature-rich electronic devices. It allows for greater integration, improved energy efficiency, and enhanced performance, enabling a wide range of applications across industries. As semiconductor technologies continue to advance, the quest for space efficiency remains at the forefront, shaping the future of electronics.

Emerging Technologies

Miniaturization has paved the way for the development of emerging technologies like Internet of Things (IoT) devices, which rely on small and energy-efficient components. Emerging technologies in Miniaturisation within semiconductor technologies are revolutionizing the electronics industry, enabling smaller, more powerful, and energy-efficient devices. These technologies are driving advancements in various fields, from mobile devices to medical implants. Let's look at some notable emerging technologies in miniaturization.

3D Integrated Circuits (3D ICs): This technology involves stacking multiple layers of circuitry on top of each other, effectively increasing the integration density and performance of chips. 3D ICs enable faster data transmission and reduced power consumption. FinFET is a type of transistor design that improves energy efficiency and reduces leakage current. It enhances the control over the flow of current, enabling higher performance while minimizing power consumption.

Quantum dots are nanoscale semiconductor particles that exhibit unique optical and electronic properties. They are used in displays, lighting, and imaging technologies, offering improved colour accuracy and energy efficiency. As transistors continue to shrink, researchers are exploring nanoscale transistors such as nanowires and nanotubes. These structures offer better control over electron flow and can lead to highly energy-efficient devices.

Materials like graphene and transition metal dichalcogenides (TMDs) are only a few atoms thick. They exhibit exceptional electrical, thermal, and mechanical properties, making them ideal for miniaturized electronic components. Inspired by the human brain, neuromorphic chips are designed to mimic neural networks. They are used in artificial intelligence applications, enabling efficient processing of complex tasks with lower power consumption.

MEMS technology integrates mechanical elements, sensors, actuators, and electronics on a single chip. It's used in various applications, from accelerometers in smartphones to pressure sensors in medical devices. Photonics involves the use of light to transmit data. Photonic integrated circuits (PICs) combine optical components and electronics on the same chip, enabling high-speed data transmission and reducing energy consumption.

These technologies enable the creation of devices that can bend, fold, or stretch without losing functionality. They are crucial for wearable technology, electronic skin, and other innovative applications. Packaging innovations, such as wafer-level packaging and chiplets, allow for more efficient stacking of components and integration of functionalities within a smaller footprint.

Microfluidic devices use tiny channels to manipulate fluids at the microscale. They have applications in medical diagnostics, drug delivery, and chemical analysis, enabling precise and efficient processes. Miniaturized devices are increasingly incorporating energy harvesting technologies that generate power from sources like ambient light, heat, or motion, reducing the need for external power sources. Miniaturisation is enabling the proliferation of IoT devices that can monitor and control various aspects of our environment, contributing to smarter homes, cities, and industries.

These emerging technologies are shaping the future of Miniaturisation in semiconductor technologies. They are enabling the development of more advanced, efficient, and versatile devices that have a profound impact on various industries and our daily lives. As these technologies continue to evolve, we can expect even greater Miniaturisation achievements and applications.

Challenges

While Miniaturisation brings numerous benefits, it also presents challenges. As transistors approach atomic scales, issues like quantum tunnelling and power leakage become more significant, necessitating innovative solutions in materials and design. While Miniaturisation in semiconductor technologies has led to remarkable advancements, it also brings forth a set of challenges that need to be addressed. As transistors become smaller, leakage current—unintended current flow when the transistor is turned off—increases. This leads to higher power dissipation, limiting the energy efficiency gains of miniaturization.

Smaller components generate heat more densely, making effective heat dissipation a challenge. Overheating can impact device performance and longevity, necessitating innovative cooling solutions. At the nanoscale, quantum effects become more pronounced. Electrons can tunnel through barriers, leading to uncertain behaviour. This requires complex modelling and design adjustments to ensure reliable device operation.

Shrinking components can result in increased vulnerability to various stressors, such as mechanical strain, temperature fluctuations, and radiation. Ensuring the reliability and durability of these tiny devices is crucial. Achieving the necessary precision for manufacturing nanoscale features is challenging. Even slight variations can lead to performance discrepancies and defects in the final product.

As Miniaturisation progresses, the yield—the percentage of functional chips per wafer—can decline due to manufacturing complexities. This can drive up production costs and impact overall affordability. As components become smaller, interconnects that carry signals between them face limitations in terms of speed, resistance, and capacitance, affecting overall performance. Moore's Law, the observation that the number of transistors on a chip doubles approximately every two years, is approaching physical limits. Smaller components could encounter quantum tunnelling issues, hindering further scaling.

Designing and optimizing nanoscale components and circuits require advanced tools and methodologies. As complexity increases, the design process becomes more intricate and time-consuming. Some materials used in traditional semiconductor manufacturing might not be suitable for Miniaturisation due to quantum effects and other factors. Developing new materials and ensuring their compatibility is a challenge.

Miniaturized components often require supporting technologies like new packaging methods and advanced manufacturing processes. Coordinating these elements into a cohesive ecosystem can be complex. Tiny components can be susceptible to security threats such as counterfeiting, tampering, and reverse engineering. Ensuring the security of these devices is vital, especially in critical applications.

The manufacturing processes involved in Miniaturisation can be resource-intensive and environmentally impactful. Developing sustainable fabrication methods is a challenge. Addressing these challenges requires collaboration among semiconductor manufacturers, researchers, and engineers. As the industry continues to innovate, solutions will emerge to overcome these obstacles and unlock the full potential of Miniaturisation in semiconductor technologies.

Manufacturing Advances

Achieving Miniaturisation requires advancements in semiconductor manufacturing techniques, including photolithography, etching, and deposition processes. Manufacturing advances have played a crucial role in enabling the Miniaturisation of semiconductor technologies. These advancements have allowed for the creation of increasingly smaller and more complex components with greater precision and efficiency. Let's look at some of the key manufacturing advances in miniaturization.

Photolithography is a fundamental process used to pattern semiconductor wafers. Advanced photolithography techniques, such as extreme ultraviolet (EUV) lithography, enable the creation of smaller features with higher resolution, enhancing the overall Miniaturisation process. To overcome the limitations of two-dimensional scaling, manufacturers have developed techniques for stacking multiple layers of transistors and components. This 3D integration allows for increased functionality and performance in a smaller footprint.

The use of new materials, such as high-k dielectrics and FinFETs (Fin Field-Effect Transistors), has improved the performance and efficiency of semiconductor devices. These materials help to mitigate some of the challenges associated with miniaturization.

ALD is a precise thin-film deposition technique that enables the controlled growth of extremely thin layers of materials. This technique is vital for creating the intricate structures required for nanoscale devices.

Ion implantation is used to introduce impurities into the semiconductor material to modify its electrical properties. Precise ion implantation techniques help control the behaviour of tiny transistors and components. CVD is a method used to deposit thin films of materials onto a substrate. It is essential for creating layers with specific properties, such as insulating or conducting characteristics.

Etching is used to remove material from the semiconductor substrate to create patterns. Advances in etching technology enable the creation of smaller features and finer details in the manufacturing process. Techniques such as wafer bonding and thinning enable the integration of different materials and the creation of thinner wafers for 3D integration and packaging.

Manufacturers are exploring methods to create large-scale integrated circuits on a single wafer. This approach reduces the need for assembly and packaging steps, streamlining the manufacturing process. Precise measurements and process control are essential in miniaturization. Advanced metrology tools help monitor and adjust manufacturing processes to ensure accuracy and consistency.

The integration of automation, robotics, and data analytics into semiconductor manufacturing enhances efficiency, reduces errors, and improves yield rates, all of which are critical for miniaturization. As the complexity of miniaturized components increases, yield management becomes more important. Techniques such as defect detection and correction are crucial for achieving high yields. These manufacturing advances have revolutionized the semiconductor industry, enabling the production of ever-smaller and more powerful devices. They have paved the way for the development of advanced electronics, from high-performance processors to compact sensors, and have been instrumental in driving innovation in various sectors.

Economic Impact

Miniaturisation has led to the creation of new markets, industries, and job opportunities related to semiconductor manufacturing, design, and applications. The Miniaturisation of semiconductor technologies has had a profound economic impact on various industries and economies worldwide. This impact can be observed across multiple dimensions.

Miniaturization has led to the development of smaller, more powerful, and energy-efficient electronic devices. This, in turn, has improved productivity in industries that rely on these technologies, such as computing, communication, healthcare, automotive, and manufacturing. Miniaturisation has enabled the creation of entirely new markets and industries. For example, the proliferation of smartphones, wearable devices, IoT (Internet of Things) sensors, and smart appliances has created opportunities for innovation and entrepreneurship.

Miniaturized semiconductor technologies have facilitated global connectivity through the widespread adoption of mobile devices, communication networks, and the internet. This has transformed the way businesses operate, interact, and reach customers worldwide. Smaller and more efficient semiconductor components often result in cost savings, as they require less raw material and energy during manufacturing. This cost reduction can trickle down to consumers through more affordable products.

The growth of industries related to miniaturized technologies, such as electronics manufacturing, design, software development, and maintenance, has led to job creation and opportunities for skilled workers. The demand for miniaturized semiconductor components has had a ripple effect throughout the supply chain, benefiting suppliers of materials, equipment, packaging, and testing services. The Miniaturisation of semiconductors has revolutionized consumer electronics. Devices like smartphones, tablets, smartwatches, and smart TVs have become integral parts of daily life, driving consumer spending and industry growth.

Miniaturized semiconductor technologies have enabled the development of medical devices, imaging equipment, and diagnostic tools that enhance patient care and medical research. The automotive sector has seen the integration of advanced miniaturized electronics for safety features, infotainment systems, autonomous driving capabilities, and energy-efficient engines. Miniaturisation has contributed to energy efficiency improvements in various industries. Energy-efficient electronics play a critical role in reducing power consumption and greenhouse gas emissions. Continued advances in Miniaturisation fuel research and development efforts in the semiconductor industry. This fosters innovation and drives technological breakthroughs across sectors. Countries that invest in semiconductor research, manufacturing, and innovation can enhance their global competitiveness by contributing to technological advancements and economic growth.

The economic impact of Miniaturisation in semiconductor technologies is far-reaching, influencing multiple sectors and economies around the world. This impact is expected to continue as innovations in Miniaturisation drive further advancements in electronics, communication, automation, and more.

Miniaturization advances have been instrumental in shaping the modern digital landscape. They have enabled the development of powerful and versatile electronic devices that have become integral to our daily lives, from smartphones to smart appliances, medical devices to autonomous vehicles. As technology continues to evolve, Miniaturisation remains a driving force behind innovation and progress in the semiconductor industry.

Nanotechnology

The development of nanoscale manufacturing techniques has allowed for the creation of transistors and other components on the nanometer scale, enabling even more efficient and compact devices. Nanotechnology has played a significant role in advancing semiconductor technologies, leading to the development of smaller, more powerful, and energy-efficient electronic devices. Let's look at some key ways in which nanotechnology has impacted semiconductor technologies.

Nanotechnology allows for the precise manipulation and arrangement of materials at the nanoscale. This level of control has enabled the creation of semiconductor components with extremely small dimensions, leading to higher integration densities and increased performance.

Improved Performance

By using nanoscale materials and structures, semiconductor devices can achieve enhanced electrical and optical properties. For example, nanoscale transistors can operate at higher speeds and with lower power consumption, leading to improved overall device performance. Improved performance is one of the key benefits that nanotechnology brings to semiconductor technologies. Lets see how nanotechnology has contributed to enhancing the performance of semiconductor devices.

Nanotechnology allows for the fabrication of smaller transistors and other components, which in turn leads to shorter electron travel distances within the device. This reduction in distance enables faster switching speeds and overall higher performance of electronic circuits. Nanoscale materials, such as high-mobility channel materials and nanowires, offer improved electron mobility. This results in better electron flow through the device, leading to faster and more efficient operation.

Nanoscale devices exhibit reduced power consumption due to their smaller dimensions. With shorter electron pathways and reduced leakage currents, energy efficiency is enhanced, contributing to improved battery life in portable devices and reduced energy consumption in larger systems. Nanotechnology enables higher levels of integration on a single chip. This means that more components, such as transistors, memory cells, and sensors, can be packed onto a single piece of silicon. This increased integration boosts device performance by allowing for more complex and capable systems.

Nanoscale materials offer unique properties that can improve performance. For example, materials like graphene and carbon nanotubes have exceptional electrical and thermal conductivity, making them ideal candidates for high-performance electronic components. At the nanoscale, quantum effects become significant. While they can be challenging to control, they also open up opportunities for creating new types of devices that operate based on quantum phenomena. Quantum dots, for instance, can be used to create ultra-sensitive sensors and efficient light-emitting devices.

Nanotechnology has facilitated the development of advanced optoelectronic devices, such as light-emitting diodes (LEDs) and photodetectors. Nanoscale materials and structures allow for precise control of light emission and detection, leading to improved performance in communication and sensing applications. Nanoscale devices can operate at higher frequencies, enabling better performance in high-speed communication systems, radar applications, and other high-frequency electronics. Nanotechnology can help reduce unwanted noise and interference in electronic circuits. By designing nanoscale components with carefully controlled properties, engineers can minimize signal degradation and enhance overall device performance.

In summary, the application of nanotechnology in semiconductor technologies has significantly improved the performance of electronic devices. By leveraging the unique properties of nanoscale materials and structures, engineers have been able to achieve faster speeds, lower power consumption, increased integration, and other performance enhancements that have transformed the capabilities of modern electronics.

Energy Efficiency

Nanotechnology has led to the development of energy-efficient semiconductor devices. Nanoscale materials and designs enable better control of electron flow and reduced energy losses, resulting in devices that consume less power. Energy efficiency is a critical aspect of semiconductor technologies, and nanotechnology has played a significant role in improving energy efficiency in various electronic devices. Let's see how nanotechnology contributes to energy efficiency.

Nanoscale components, such as transistors and memory cells, have smaller dimensions, resulting in shorter electron pathways. This leads to reduced power consumption since electrons need to travel shorter distances, minimizing energy losses due to resistance. Nanoscale materials and structures exhibit lower leakage currents compared to their larger counterparts. This is particularly important for maintaining energy efficiency in standby or idle modes, as lower leakage currents result in less power wastage. Nanotechnology allows for the design of materials with enhanced thermal conductivity, which is crucial for effective heat dissipation. Efficient heat management prevents overheating and ensures that devices can operate optimally without consuming excess energy.

Nanotechnology has enabled the development of energy-harvesting devices that can convert ambient energy sources, such as light, heat, or vibration, into usable electrical energy. These devices can power sensors and low-power electronics without the need for external power sources. Nanotechnology has revolutionized the field of light-emitting diodes (LEDs). Nanoscale materials, such as quantum dots, allow for precise control of the colour and efficiency of emitted light. This results in energy-efficient lighting solutions that consume less power and have a longer lifespan.

Nanotechnology has led to advancements in solar cell technologies. Nanostructured materials can enhance light absorption, enable efficient charge separation, and increase the overall efficiency of photovoltaic devices, leading to improved energy conversion from sunlight. Nanotechnology has impacted energy storage solutions, including batteries and supercapacitors. Nanomaterials can enhance the charge and discharge rates of batteries, increase their energy density, and improve overall efficiency in energy storage systems.

Nanotechnology has facilitated the development of thin-film electronic devices with reduced material usage. These devices are lightweight and consume less energy during production, making them more environmentally friendly and energy-efficient. Nanoscale sensors and actuators are more energy-efficient and responsive, enabling better monitoring and control of systems. This is crucial for applications such as smart buildings, industrial automation, and environmental monitoring. Nanotechnology has paved the way for energy-efficient wearable devices by enabling compact and power-efficient components. Wearable health monitors, fitness trackers, and smartwatches benefit from energy-efficient nanoscale sensors and low-power processing units.

In summary, nanotechnology has had a transformative impact on energy efficiency in semiconductor technologies. By leveraging nanoscale materials and engineering techniques, electronics have become more power-efficient, contributing to longer battery life, reduced energy consumption, and the development of sustainable technologies.

Novel Materials

Nanotechnology has introduced new materials with unique properties that can be integrated into semiconductor devices. For instance, quantum dots and nanowires are used to create innovative optoelectronic components, such as LEDs and photodetectors.

Nanotechnology has introduced novel materials that have revolutionized semiconductor technologies, leading to enhanced performance, energy efficiency, and new functionalities. Let's see some of the novel materials used in nanotechnology for semiconductor applications. These are thin, elongated structures with diameters on the nanometer scale. Nanowires are used in various applications, including transistors, sensors, and photodetectors, due to their excellent electrical and optical properties.

Quantum dots are nanoscale semiconductor particles that exhibit unique electronic and optical properties. They can emit light of specific colours based on their size, making them valuable for displays, LEDs, and biological imaging. Graphene is a single layer of carbon atoms arranged in a two-dimensional honeycomb lattice. It has exceptional electrical and thermal conductivity, making it suitable for high-speed transistors, flexible electronics, and transparent conductive films.

These are cylindrical carbon structures with extraordinary mechanical, electrical, and thermal properties. Carbon nanotubes find applications in transistors, sensors, and nanoscale interconnects. Besides graphene, other two-dimensional materials like transition metal dichalcogenides (TMDs) have gained attention. TMDs offer diverse electrical and optical properties, enabling their use in electronics, optoelectronics, and energy storage.

Nanoparticles are incorporated into polymers, metals, or ceramics to create nanocomposites with improved properties. These materials find applications in flexible electronics, coatings, and high-strength materials. Nanoparticles exhibit unique properties due to their small size and high surface area. They are used in various semiconductor devices, such as transistors, photodetectors, and solar cells, to enhance performance. Organic semiconductors are carbon-based materials with tuneable electronic properties. They are used in flexible electronics, OLED displays, and organic solar cells.

Perovskite materials have gained attention in solar cell technology due to their excellent light absorption and cost-effectiveness. They offer a potential solution for efficient and low-cost photovoltaic devices. These materials conduct electricity on their surfaces while insulating in their interiors. They hold promise for energy-efficient electronics, quantum computing, and spintronics. Ferroelectrics exhibit reversible polarization switching under an applied electric field. They are utilized in memory devices and energy storage applications.

Magnetic nanoparticles are used in data storage, sensors, and medical applications. They enable non-volatile memory and improved data storage density. Plasmonic materials exhibit strong interactions with light, leading to applications in sensors, enhanced spectroscopy, and photothermal therapy. These materials undergo reversible phase transitions between crystalline and amorphous states. They are used in non-volatile memory and optical data storage. These novel materials are driving innovations in nanotechnology and semiconductor industries. Their unique properties and functionalities enable the development of advanced electronic devices with improved performance, energy efficiency, and miniaturization.

Quantum Effects

At the nanoscale, quantum effects become more pronounced, and these effects can be harnessed for various applications. Quantum dots, for example, exhibit size-dependent optical and electronic properties that are exploited in quantum computing and quantum communication.

Quantum effects play a crucial role in nanotechnology and semiconductor technologies, especially as devices continue to shrink to nanoscale dimensions. These effects, which arise from the behaviour of particles at the quantum level, can significantly impact the behaviour and performance of semiconductor devices. Let's look at some key quantum effects in nanotechnology. As semiconductor devices are miniaturized to nanoscale dimensions, quantum confinement becomes prominent. This effect limits the movement of electrons and holes within the material, leading to changes in their energy levels and properties. Quantum dots and nanowires are examples of structures where quantum confinement is exploited to create unique electronic and optical properties.

Quantum tunnelling allows particles to pass through energy barriers that classical physics would predict as impassable. In semiconductor devices, tunnelling is used in tunnel diodes and quantum tunnelling transistors, enabling new functionalities such as low-power switching and memory storage. Quantum dots are nanoscale semiconductor particles that exhibit discrete energy levels due to their small size. These energy levels result in unique optical properties, including size-tuneable emission colours. Quantum dots are used in displays, LEDs, solar cells, and biological imaging.

Quantum interference occurs when the probability amplitudes of different quantum states interfere with each other, leading to constructive or destructive interference. This effect is exploited in quantum well structures to engineer electronic properties and improve device performance. Spintronics exploits the intrinsic spin of electrons in addition to their charge. Quantum mechanical effects related to spin, such as spin coherence and quantum tunnelling of spin states, are harnessed to create spin-based devices for data storage and logic operations.

Quantum computers leverage the superposition and entanglement of quantum bits (qubits) to perform calculations that are practically impossible for classical computers. Quantum effects enable the creation of qubits and their manipulation, paving the way for advanced computing capabilities. The Quantum Hall Effect occurs in two-dimensional electron systems subjected to a strong magnetic field. It leads to quantization of the Hall resistance and offers a highly precise standard for resistance measurements. In nanoscale structures, such as quantum dots or single-electron transistors, the discrete nature of charge carriers can lead to single-electron tunnelling events. These effects are used for ultra-sensitive charge sensing and manipulation.

Entanglement is a phenomenon where the quantum states of two or more particles become correlated in such a way that the state of one cannot be described independently of the state of the others. Entanglement is exploited in quantum communication and quantum cryptography. Quantum effects are used in sensors that can achieve high sensitivity by exploiting the quantum properties of particles. Examples include quantum optical sensors and quantum-enhanced magnetometers.

Quantum effects in nanotechnology and semiconductor technologies enable the development of novel devices, enhanced functionalities, and breakthrough applications that are not achievable using classical physics alone. As technology continues to advance, harnessing these effects will become increasingly important for driving innovation in various industries.

Sensing and Detection

Nanotechnology has enabled the development of highly sensitive sensors and detectors. Nanoscale materials can detect specific molecules or particles with high accuracy, making them valuable tools in medical diagnostics, environmental monitoring, and more. Sensing and detection are critical aspects of nanotechnology and semiconductor technologies, enabling the creation of highly sensitive and efficient devices for various applications. Nanoscale sensors and detectors take advantage of the unique properties of nanomaterials and quantum effects to achieve enhanced sensitivity, selectivity, and responsiveness. Here is an overview of sensing and detection in nanotechnology.

Nanoscale sensors utilize nanomaterials, such as nanoparticles, nanowires, and nanotubes, to detect specific molecules or environmental changes. These sensors can detect a wide range of substances, including gases, chemicals, biomolecules, and pathogens. Due to their small size and high surface area, nanoscale sensors offer increased sensitivity and rapid response times. Quantum sensors leverage quantum properties, such as superposition and entanglement, to achieve ultra-high sensitivity. Examples include quantum-enhanced magnetometers, gravimeters, and atomic sensors. Quantum sensors can surpass the limitations of classical sensors in measuring weak signals and small changes.

Nanomechanical sensors utilize the mechanical properties of nanoscale structures, such as cantilevers or resonators, to detect changes in mass or force. These sensors are used in applications like chemical sensing, biomolecule detection, and environmental monitoring. Plasmonic sensors rely on the interaction between light and surface plasmons (collective oscillations of electrons) in metal nanostructures. Changes in the surrounding environment lead to shifts in plasmon resonance, allowing detection of molecular binding events or changes in refractive index.

Nanoelectronic sensors exploit changes in electrical properties, such as conductivity or resistance, due to interactions with analytes. Nanowire-based field-effect transistors (FETs) and other nanoelectronic devices are used for sensitive detection of various targets. Biosensors combine biological molecules (such as antibodies or DNA) with nanomaterials to detect specific biomolecules. They find applications in medical diagnostics, environmental monitoring, and food safety.

Nanotechnology enables the development of highly selective and sensitive gas sensors for detecting gases such as carbon dioxide, methane, and volatile organic compounds. These sensors have applications in environmental monitoring, industrial safety, and healthcare. Nanotechnology enhances imaging and spectroscopic techniques, enabling the visualization of materials and biological structures at nanoscale resolution. Scanning probe microscopes, super-resolution microscopy, and surface-enhanced Raman spectroscopy (SERS) are examples of nanoscale imaging and spectroscopic tools. Nanosensors play a crucial role in environmental monitoring, helping detect pollutants, toxins, and contaminants in air, water, and soil.

Nanotechnology-enabled sensors are used in medical diagnostics for detecting biomarkers associated with diseases. They enable early disease detection, personalized medicine, and point-of-care testing. Nanosensors are integrated into IoT devices, enabling real-time data collection and communication for applications like smart cities, agriculture, and healthcare.

Incorporating nanotechnology into sensing and detection technologies has revolutionized our ability to monitor and analyse various parameters in a precise and efficient manner. As nanotechnology continues to advance, the development of even more sophisticated and versatile sensors and detectors is expected, further expanding their applications and impact across industries.

Memory Storage

Nanotechnology has led to advancements in non-volatile memory technologies, such as flash memory and resistive random-access memory (RRAM). These technologies offer higher data storage densities and faster read/write speeds.

Memory storage is a crucial component of nanotechnology and semiconductor technologies, driving the development of smaller, faster, and more efficient data storage devices. Nanotechnology has played a significant role in pushing the boundaries of memory storage capabilities, enabling the creation of high-density, non-volatile, and energy-efficient memory devices. An overview of memory storage in nanotechnology is as follows.

Nanotechnology has led to the development of memory devices at the nanoscale level. These devices use nanomaterials, such as nanoparticles, nanowires, and nanotubes, to store and retrieve data. Nanoscale memory devices offer advantages like high storage density, low power consumption, and faster data access. Flash memory is a type of non-volatile memory commonly used in consumer electronics. Nanoscale fabrication techniques have allowed for the Miniaturisation of flash memory cells, resulting in higher storage capacities and improved performance.

PCM is a type of memory that relies on the reversible phase transition of a material between amorphous and crystalline states. Nanoscale control of phase change materials enables faster switching times and higher storage density. RRAM is a nanoscale memory technology that utilizes the resistance switching behaviour of certain materials. It offers fast write and read speeds, low power consumption, and scalability.

MRAM uses the magnetic properties of materials to store data. Nanotechnology has enabled the fabrication of nanoscale magnetic tunnel junctions, leading to higher storage densities and improved performance. Nanotechnology has facilitated the development of 3D memory stacking, where memory layers are stacked on top of each other to increase storage capacity without increasing the footprint.

Quantum dots, nanoscale semiconductor particles, have been explored for use in memory storage. They can store information as discrete energy states, offering potential for high-density data storage. Neuromorphic memory devices are inspired by the human brain's ability to process information. Nanotechnology enables the creation of memristors and other devices that can emulate synaptic behaviour, paving the way for advanced artificial intelligence applications. Nanotechnology has contributed to the development of non-volatile memory technologies, where data remains stored even when power is turned off. This is crucial for energy-efficient and reliable data storage.

Nanotechnology-enabled memory devices often consume less power, making them energy-efficient options for various applications, including mobile devices, data centres, and Internet of Things (IoT) devices. Nanotechnology has enabled the integration of memory and logic devices on a single chip, leading to improved data processing and reduced latency.

The continuous advancement of nanotechnology in memory storage is driving innovations in various industries, from consumer electronics to cloud computing. As researchers explore novel materials, design techniques, and fabrication methods, memory storage devices are becoming increasingly efficient, reliable, and capable of meeting the demands of the digital age.

Flexible Electronics

Nanotechnology has enabled the creation of flexible and wearable electronics. Nanomaterials can be integrated into flexible substrates, allowing for the development of bendable and stretchable devices. Flexible electronics is a groundbreaking field within nanotechnology and semiconductor technologies that focuses on creating electronic devices and circuits that are not only functional but also bendable, stretchable, and conformable. This innovation has the potential to revolutionize various industries by enabling the development of flexible displays, wearable devices, medical sensors, and more. The following is an overview of flexible electronics in nanotechnology.

Nanotechnology plays a crucial role in developing nanomaterials that exhibit unique mechanical and electrical properties. Nanomaterials like carbon nanotubes, graphene, and conductive polymers are used to create flexible electronic components. Flexible thin-film transistors are fundamental building blocks of flexible electronics. Nanotechnology allows for the fabrication of nanoscale semiconductor materials and thin films that can be integrated into bendable substrates.

Organic materials, such as organic semiconductors and conductive polymers, are key to flexible electronics.

Nanotechnology enables the precise control of molecular structures, improving the performance and flexibility of organic electronic devices. Nanotechnology has led to the development of flexible displays that can be rolled up or bent without affecting their functionality. These displays use nanoscale materials to create flexible pixels and conductive layers.

Flexible electronics are integral to wearable devices like smartwatches, fitness trackers, and medical sensors. Nanoscale components make these devices lightweight, comfortable, and capable of conforming to the wearer's body. Nanotechnology-enabled flexible sensors can be integrated into clothing or medical devices to monitor vital signs, glucose levels, and other health parameters. These sensors offer non-invasive monitoring for improved healthcare.

Flexible electronics enable the creation of IoT devices with unique form factors. These devices can be seamlessly integrated into various environments, from smart homes to industrial settings. Nanotechnology is used to develop flexible energy-harvesting devices that can generate power from motion, vibrations, or light. These devices provide a sustainable energy source for wearable electronics. Nanotechnology allows for roll-to-roll manufacturing processes, enabling large-scale production of flexible electronics. This scalable fabrication method is crucial for commercializing flexible devices. Despite the progress, challenges remain, such as maintaining performance while ensuring flexibility, achieving high reliability, and developing cost-effective manufacturing methods. Researchers are continually advancing the field through innovations in materials, fabrication techniques, and device architectures.

Flexible electronics have the potential to impact industries such as consumer electronics, healthcare, automotive, aerospace, and more. They offer new design possibilities, improved user experiences, and novel applications. As nanotechnology continues to evolve, flexible electronics will likely become even more versatile, integrating seamlessly into our daily lives. Advancements in nanomaterials, device architectures, and manufacturing processes will drive the field forward.

Flexible electronics in nanotechnology are opening up new frontiers of innovation, allowing for the creation of electronic devices that were once deemed impossible. The convergence of nanotechnology and flexible electronics holds the promise of a more connected, flexible, and personalized technological future.

Advanced Manufacturing Techniques

Nanotechnology has driven the development of advanced manufacturing techniques, such as nanoimprint lithography and atomic layer deposition. These techniques enable the precise fabrication of nanoscale structures. Advanced manufacturing techniques play a crucial role in the field of nanotechnology and semiconductor technologies, enabling the precise fabrication and assembly of nanoscale components and structures. These techniques are essential for realizing the potential of nanomaterials and nanodevices in various applications, from electronics to medicine. Let's look at some advanced manufacturing techniques used in nanotechnology.

Nanolithography involves the patterning of nanoscale features on a substrate. Techniques like electron beam lithography, extreme ultraviolet lithography, and nanoimprint lithography enable the creation of intricate patterns with high resolution. ALD is a thin-film deposition technique that allows for precise control of material growth at the atomic level. It is used to create conformal and uniform thin films for various applications, including semiconductor devices. MBE is a technique used to grow thin films of materials with atomic precision. It's commonly used to create semiconductor structures, quantum dots, and other nanoscale devices. CVD is used to deposit thin films of materials onto a substrate by chemical reactions in a gas phase.

It's widely used for growing nanomaterials like graphene, carbon nanotubes, and semiconductor nanowires.

This technique involves creating patterns on a substrate by pressing it onto a mould with nanoscale features. It's a cost-effective way to replicate complex nanostructures. Self-assembly techniques leverage molecular forces to spontaneously arrange nanoscale components into desired structures. This approach is inspired by natural processes and can be used to create ordered arrays of nanoparticles. Directed self-assembly involves using guiding templates or patterns to direct the self-assembly of nanoscale components. It's used to create intricate structures and devices. Nanomanipulation techniques use tools like atomic force microscopes (AFMs) or electron microscopes to manipulate individual atoms or molecules. This is crucial for building nanoscale structures with high precision.

Additive manufacturing techniques, including 3D printing, can be adapted for nanoscale fabrication. Nanoscale 3D printing enables the creation of complex and customized structures with precise dimensions. Soft lithography involves using elastomeric stamps to create patterns on substrates. It's used for fabricating microfluidic devices, biomimetic structures, and more. Templated growth techniques use pre-existing patterns as templates for the growth of nanoscale structures. An example is the use of porous templates for creating nanowires.

These approaches refer to building structures from the bottom up (assembling individual atoms or molecules) or from the top down (carving or etching away material). A combination of both approaches is often used for complex nanofabrication. These advanced manufacturing techniques enable the creation of nanoscale structures with unprecedented precision and control. They are essential for realizing the potential of nanotechnology in various fields, from electronics and energy to medicine and materials science. As these techniques continue to evolve, they will contribute to the development of innovative and transformative technologies.

Future Trends

Nanotechnology continues to drive innovation in semiconductor technologies. As the industry faces challenges related to Moore's Law and the limits of conventional lithography, nanotechnology offers new avenues for achieving further Miniaturisation and performance enhancements.

Memory storage is a crucial component of nanotechnology and semiconductor technologies, driving the development of smaller, faster, and more efficient data storage devices. Nanotechnology has played a significant role in pushing the boundaries of memory storage capabilities, enabling the creation of high-density, non-volatile, and energy-efficient memory devices. This is an overview of memory storage in nanotechnology.

Nanotechnology has led to the development of memory devices at the nanoscale level. These devices use nanomaterials, such as nanoparticles, nanowires, and nanotubes, to store and retrieve data. Nanoscale memory devices offer advantages like high storage density, low power consumption, and faster data access. Flash memory is a type of non-volatile memory commonly used in consumer electronics. Nanoscale fabrication techniques have allowed for the Miniaturisation of flash memory cells, resulting in higher storage capacities and improved performance.

PCM is a type of memory that relies on the reversible phase transition of a material between amorphous and crystalline states. Nanoscale control of phase change materials enables faster switching times and higher storage density. RRAM is a nanoscale memory technology that utilizes the resistance switching behaviour of certain materials. It offers fast write and read speeds, low power consumption, and scalability.

MRAM uses the magnetic properties of materials to store data. Nanotechnology has enabled the fabrication of nanoscale magnetic tunnel junctions, leading to higher storage densities and improved performance. Nanotechnology has facilitated the development of 3D memory stacking, where memory layers are stacked on top of each other to increase storage capacity without increasing the footprint. Quantum dots, nanoscale semiconductor particles, have been explored for use in memory storage. They can store information as discrete energy states, offering potential for high-density data storage. Neuromorphic memory devices are inspired by the human brain's ability to process information. Nanotechnology enables the creation of memristors and other devices that can emulate synaptic behaviour, paving the way for advanced artificial intelligence applications.

Nanotechnology has contributed to the development of non-volatile memory technologies, where data remains stored even when power is turned off. This is crucial for energy-efficient and reliable data storage. Nanotechnology-enabled memory devices often consume less power, making them energy-efficient options for various applications, including mobile devices, data centres, and Internet of Things (IoT) devices. Nanotechnology has enabled the integration of memory and logic devices on a single chip, leading to improved data processing and reduced latency.

The continuous advancement of nanotechnology in memory storage is driving innovations in various industries, from consumer electronics to cloud computing. As researchers explore novel materials, design techniques, and fabrication methods, memory storage devices are becoming increasingly efficient, reliable, and capable of meeting the demands of the digital age.

Nanotechnology has revolutionized semiconductor technologies by providing the tools and methods to manipulate materials and structures at the atomic and molecular level. This has led to breakthroughs in device performance, energy efficiency, and novel applications that have transformed the electronics industry.

Future trends in nanotechnology and semiconductor technologies hold the promise of revolutionizing various industries, from electronics and healthcare to energy and materials science. These are some key trends to watch for. Nanotechnology will play a crucial role in advancing quantum computing. Quantum bits (qubits) can be implemented using nanoscale devices, such as superconducting circuits and trapped ions, leading to unprecedented computational power. As traditional silicon-based electronics approach their limits, nanoelectronics offer solutions. Nanoscale transistors, tunnelling devices, and spintronics will enable faster and more energy-efficient electronic devices.

Nanotechnology will continue to transform medicine with targeted drug delivery, imaging agents, and minimally invasive treatments. Nanoscale sensors and devices will enable early disease detection and personalized therapies. Nanomaterials will enhance energy storage and conversion technologies. Nanostructured materials can improve the efficiency of batteries, supercapacitors, and solar cells, enabling more sustainable energy solutions.

Nanotechnology will drive the development of wearable devices with improved performance and comfort. Flexible electronics using nanoscale materials will find applications in health monitoring, smart textiles, and more. Nanosensors will enable real-time monitoring of environmental parameters, health conditions, and structural integrity. These sensors will be integrated into the IoT ecosystem, providing valuable data for decision-making.

Nanotechnology will lead to the development of stronger, lighter, and more durable materials. Nanocomposites and nanocoatings will enhance the performance of construction materials, aerospace components, and more. Nanoscale optical components will enable ultra-fast data communication, high-resolution imaging, and advanced sensing. Plasmonic and photonic nanomaterials will revolutionize optics and photonics.

Nanotechnology will contribute to pollution control, water purification, and sustainable agriculture. Nanomaterials can remove contaminants, enhance catalytic processes, and improve resource efficiency. Advances in nanoscale 3D printing and additive manufacturing techniques will allow for the creation of complex nanoscale structures with precision, opening up new possibilities in electronics, optics, and medicine.

Nanoscale robots and machines will be developed for tasks such as targeted drug delivery, tissue repair, and environmental monitoring. These devices will operate at the molecular level, offering unprecedented control and precision. As nanotechnology becomes more integrated into everyday life, ethical considerations and safety assessments will become paramount. Regulations and standards will be developed to ensure the responsible use of nanotechnology. Nanotechnology's future holds immense potential to transform industries, improve human health, and address global challenges. However, it's important to address ethical, environmental, and safety concerns while realizing the benefits

of these technological advancements.

Flexible electronics

Flexible electronics is a groundbreaking field within nanotechnology and semiconductor technologies that focuses on creating electronic devices and circuits that are not only functional but also bendable, stretchable, and conformable. This innovation has the potential to revolutionize various industries by enabling the development of flexible displays, wearable devices, medical sensors, and more. This is an overview of flexible electronics in nanotechnology.

Nanotechnology plays a crucial role in developing nanomaterials that exhibit unique mechanical and electrical properties. Nanomaterials like carbon nanotubes, graphene, and conductive polymers are used to create flexible electronic components. Flexible thin-film transistors are fundamental building blocks of flexible electronics. Nanotechnology allows for the fabrication of nanoscale semiconductor materials and thin films that can be integrated into bendable substrates.

Organic materials, such as organic semiconductors and conductive polymers, are key to flexible electronics. Nanotechnology enables the precise control of molecular structures, improving the performance and flexibility of organic electronic devices. Nanotechnology has led to the development of flexible displays that can be rolled up or bent without affecting their functionality. These displays use nanoscale materials to create flexible pixels and conductive layers.

Flexible electronics are integral to wearable devices like smartwatches, fitness trackers, and medical sensors. Nanoscale components make these devices lightweight, comfortable, and capable of conforming to the wearer's body. Nanotechnology-enabled flexible sensors can be integrated into clothing or medical devices to monitor vital signs, glucose levels, and other health parameters. These sensors offer non-invasive monitoring for improved healthcare.

Flexible electronics enable the creation of IoT devices with unique form factors. These devices can be seamlessly integrated into various environments, from smart homes to industrial settings. Nanotechnology is used to develop flexible energy-harvesting devices that can generate power from motion, vibrations, or light. These devices provide a sustainable energy source for wearable electronics. Nanotechnology allows for roll-to-roll manufacturing processes, enabling large-scale production of flexible electronics. This scalable fabrication method is crucial for commercializing flexible devices.

Despite the progress, challenges remain, such as maintaining performance while ensuring flexibility, achieving high reliability, and developing cost-effective manufacturing methods. Researchers are continually advancing the field through innovations in materials, fabrication techniques, and device architectures. Flexible electronics have the potential to impact industries such as consumer electronics, healthcare, automotive, aerospace, and more. They offer new design possibilities, improved user experiences, and novel applications.

As nanotechnology continues to evolve, flexible electronics will likely become even more versatile, integrating seamlessly into our daily lives. Advancements in nanomaterials, device architectures, and manufacturing processes will drive the field forward. Flexible electronics in nanotechnology are opening up new frontiers of innovation, allowing for the creation of electronic devices that were once deemed impossible. The convergence of nanotechnology and flexible electronics holds the promise of a more connected, flexible, and personalized technological future.

Advanced manufacturing techniques

Advanced manufacturing techniques play a crucial role in the field of nanotechnology and semiconductor technologies, enabling the precise fabrication and assembly of nanoscale components and structures. These techniques are essential for realizing the potential of nanomaterials and nanodevices in various applications, from electronics to medicine. These are some advanced manufacturing techniques used in nanotechnology.

Nanolithography involves the patterning of nanoscale features on a substrate. Techniques like electron beam lithography, extreme ultraviolet lithography, and nanoimprint lithography enable the creation of intricate patterns with high resolution. ALD is a thin-film deposition technique that allows for precise control of material growth at the atomic level. It is used to create conformal and uniform thin films for various applications, including semiconductor devices.

MBE is a technique used to grow thin films of materials with atomic precision. It's commonly used to create semiconductor structures, quantum dots, and other nanoscale devices. CVD is used to deposit thin films of materials onto a substrate by chemical reactions in a gas phase. It's widely used for growing nanomaterials like graphene, carbon nanotubes, and semiconductor nanowires.

This technique involves creating patterns on a substrate by pressing it onto a mould with nanoscale features. It's a cost-effective way to replicate complex nanostructures. Self-assembly techniques leverage molecular forces to spontaneously arrange nanoscale components into desired structures. This approach is inspired by natural processes and can be used to create ordered arrays of nanoparticles.

Directed self-assembly involves using guiding templates or patterns to direct the self-assembly of nanoscale components. It's used to create intricate structures and devices. Nanomanipulation techniques use tools like atomic force microscopes (AFMs) or electron microscopes to manipulate individual atoms or molecules. This is crucial for building nanoscale structures with high precision.

Additive manufacturing techniques, including 3D printing, can be adapted for nanoscale fabrication. Nanoscale 3D printing enables the creation of complex and customized structures with precise dimensions. Soft lithography involves using elastomeric stamps to create patterns on substrates. It's used for fabricating microfluidic devices, biomimetic structures, and more.

Templated growth techniques use pre-existing patterns as templates for the growth of nanoscale structures. An example is the use of porous templates for creating nanowires. These approaches refer to building structures from the bottom up (assembling individual atoms or molecules) or from the top down (carving or etching away material). A combination of both approaches is often used for complex nanofabrication.

These advanced manufacturing techniques enable the creation of nanoscale structures with unprecedented precision and control. They are essential for realizing the potential of nanotechnology in various fields, from electronics and energy to medicine and materials science. As these techniques continue to evolve, they will contribute to the development of innovative and transformative technologies.

3D Chip Stacking

Instead of just shrinking components, 3D chip stacking involves layering chips on top of each other. This increases computing power and reduces the distance signals need to travel. 3D chip stacking, also known as 3D integration, is a cutting-edge technique in semiconductor technologies that involves stacking multiple layers of chips or dies vertically on top of each other. This approach contrasts with traditional 2D chip design, where components are laid out side by side on a single plane. 3D chip stacking offers numerous advantages and has the potential to revolutionize the semiconductor industry. Let's look at some of the advantages of 3D chip stacking.

Space Efficiency

3D stacking allows components to be densely packed in a vertical arrangement, conserving valuable physical space. This is especially important as chip dimensions continue to shrink, and electronic devices demand more functionality in smaller form factors. 3D chip stacking involves layering semiconductor components vertically, utilizing the third dimension (height) for integration rather than only the traditional horizontal plane. This stacking enables more components to occupy a smaller physical footprint, enhancing space efficiency. With the ability to stack multiple layers of chips, the overall chip density increases. This translates to fitting more transistors, memory cells, and other functionalities into a smaller area, optimizing space utilization in electronic devices.

By vertically stacking chips, electronic devices can be made more compact without compromising performance. This is particularly beneficial in applications where space is at a premium, such as mobile devices, wearables, and IoT (Internet of Things) devices. In traditional 2D chip layouts, interconnects between components can take up substantial space. With 3D chip stacking, interconnects become more compact and shorter, reducing the overall area required for routing connections.

Efficient 3D chip stacking designs often include improved heat dissipation mechanisms due to shorter interconnects, reducing the need for large heat-spreading areas. Moreover, the reduced distances between components lead to energy efficiency gains. 3D chip stacking allows for different types of chips to be stacked together, enabling a system-on-chip (SoC) approach, where diverse functionalities are combined in a compact space. This technology enables the creation of customized solutions for specific applications by stacking components that are specifically tailored to meet the requirements of the device, optimizing space and performance. The space efficiency achieved through 3D chip stacking has been crucial in meeting the demand for smaller, more powerful, and energy-efficient electronic devices.

It's an ongoing area of innovation and development within the semiconductor industry, aiming to continually improve space utilization while maintaining or enhancing performance.

Higher Performance

Stacking chips vertically reduces the distance between components, resulting in shorter interconnects and faster signal transmission. This leads to improved speed and reduced latency, enhancing overall performance. 3D chip stacking allows for more transistors to be packed into a smaller area by vertically layering components. This increased transistor density significantly boosts the processing power and performance of the chips.

Traditional 2D chip layouts necessitate longer interconnects between components, leading to signal delays and reduced performance. 3D chip stacking minimizes interconnect lengths by stacking components vertically, thereby reducing signal propagation delays and enhancing speed. With the vertical stacking of chips, data can move between layers more rapidly, as the distance the data needs to travel is reduced. This results in faster data transmission and improved overall processing speed.

By stacking memory and processing components closer together, 3D chip stacking enables more efficient parallel processing, as data can move vertically between layers, facilitating simultaneous processing tasks. 3D chip stacking allows for specialized layers with distinct functionalities to be placed in proximity to each other, optimizing performance. For instance, a processor, memory, and other specialized layers can be stacked, enhancing overall efficiency and reducing bottlenecks.

While enhancing performance, 3D chip stacking has also contributed to better power management. The reduced distances for data transmission lead to lower power consumption, thereby improving overall energy efficiency. Different types of chips can be stacked together, resulting in heterogeneous integration. This facilitates the combination of various functionalities, such as processors, memory, sensors, and specialized accelerators, leading to improved overall performance. Ongoing advancements in packaging technologies associated with 3D chip stacking, such as Through-Silicon Vias (TSVs) and micro-bumps, enable better performance by optimizing connectivity and heat dissipation.

These advances in 3D chip stacking have significantly improved the performance of semiconductor devices, resulting in faster, more efficient, and powerful electronic systems across various applications, including high-performance computing, mobile devices, artificial intelligence, and more. Continual research and development in this field aim to further enhance the performance capabilities of semiconductor devices.

Power Efficiency

Shorter interconnects in 3D stacks result in lower power consumption and reduced signal degradation, as there is less resistance and capacitance to overcome. With 3D chip stacking, the vertical integration of components reduces the distances data must travel between layers. Shorter interconnects result in reduced signal propagation distances, which, in turn, decrease power consumption. 3D chip stacking allows for more efficient heat dissipation. By stacking components vertically, heat can be dissipated more effectively, which prevents overheating and reduces the need for excessive power consumption due to cooling requirements.

Reduced signal propagation distances and improved interconnects in 3D chip stacking lead to lower voltage requirements for data transmission, which contributes to power efficiency. Designing specific layers or components within the stack for low power consumption can improve the overall power efficiency of the device. For instance, having dedicated layers for power management or low-power processing can enhance energy efficiency.

3D chip stacking facilitates more granular control of voltage and frequency for individual layers or components, allowing for dynamic adjustments based on workload, further optimizing power usage. Stacking different types of chips enables the integration of specialized, low-power components, such as sensors or low-power processors. This allows for optimized power usage in various functionalities within a device.

The vertical integration in 3D chip stacking leads to a reduction in energy losses and better energy proportionality, meaning that the energy consumed is more directly proportional to the computational tasks being performed. Through-Silicon Vias (TSVs) and other advanced packaging technologies used in 3D chip stacking allow for better thermal management and signal transmission, leading to reduced power consumption. These advancements in 3D chip stacking technology have played a vital role in enhancing the power efficiency of electronic devices, making them more energy-efficient and enabling longer battery life in portable devices.

Increased Functionality

Different chip layers can be optimized for specific tasks. For example, memory chips can be stacked on top of processors, allowing for faster data access and reducing the need to transfer data between separate chips. 3D chip stacking enables the integration of various types of chips, such as processors, memory, sensors, and specialized accelerators, in a single stack. This results in increased functionality by combining diverse functionalities into a more compact space. By vertically stacking chips with specialized functionalities in close proximity, devices can perform a broader range of tasks within a smaller form factor. For instance, combining logic, memory, and sensor components in a 3D stack enhances the device's functionality.

3D chip stacking allows for more capabilities to be packed into a smaller physical space. This has been particularly valuable in mobile devices, wearables, and IoT devices, where space is limited, yet demand for functionality is high. With 3D chip stacking, different components of an SoC can be stacked in layers, enabling efficient, customized designs with a range of integrated functionalities. This enhances the overall functionality of the device.

Manufacturers can create specific layers dedicated to particular functions (e.g., processing, memory, or sensor functions), optimizing and enhancing the overall functionality of the device. Vertical stacking shortens the distance that data needs to travel within a device, reducing latency and enabling faster data transfer. This results in devices being more responsive and capable of handling complex tasks efficiently.

Devices can incorporate various functionalities, such as AI processing, graphics rendering, and high-speed data processing, within the same compact structure, enhancing the overall capabilities of the device. 3D chip stacking allows for customization to suit specific application requirements, integrating tailored functionalities into a single package. This results in devices that are optimized for specific uses. The increased functionality resulting from 3D chip stacking has had a significant impact on electronic devices, enabling them to perform a wider range of tasks efficiently within a smaller space.

Thermal Management

Stacking chips vertically provides more surface area for heat dissipation, aiding in thermal management. This is crucial as heat dissipation becomes a challenge with smaller chip sizes and higher power densities. Shorter interconnects in vertically stacked 3D chips minimize the distance data needs to travel, reducing the heat generated due to signal propagation. Shorter pathways result in lower resistance, decreasing power loss and, consequently, heat generation.

These vertical interconnections used in 3D chip stacking enable efficient heat dissipation by acting as pathways for heat to travel from one layer to another. They also aid in reducing the thermal resistance between layers. The close proximity of components in 3D stacking enables better heat conduction, as the heat generated by one layer can be conducted and dissipated through adjacent layers efficiently, reducing hotspots.

Advanced materials and designs for thermal interface layers improve the conduction of heat between stacked chips, aiding in the dissipation of heat from the components to the cooling systems. Innovative cooling solutions, such as microfluidic channels or embedded micro-cooling systems, can be integrated into the 3D chip stack to manage and remove heat effectively.

Designing chips with thermal considerations in mind allows for optimal placement of heat-generating components, helping to minimize hotspots and improve overall thermal performance. Advanced computer-aided modelling and simulation techniques help engineers predict and optimize thermal performance during the design phase, ensuring effective heat management in 3D chip stacking. Dynamic power and clock gating techniques employed in 3D chip stacking reduce power consumption and subsequent heat generation in idle or less active components.

Heterogeneous Integration

Different types of chips, such as logic, memory, sensors, and communication modules, can be stacked together, enabling heterogeneous integration. This promotes diverse functionalities within a single package.

3D chip stacking enables the integration of diverse functionalities, such as processors, memory, sensors, RF components, and specialized accelerators, into a single stacked package. This amalgamation of various technologies into one system-on-chip (SoC) optimizes performance and functionality.

By stacking different types of chips in close proximity, each optimized for specific functions, overall performance is enhanced. For instance, combining logic, memory, and specialized accelerators can result in an optimized and efficient system.

Heterogeneous integration in 3D chip stacking allows for a higher level of Miniaturisation and space utilization within a device. This is particularly valuable in applications where compactness is critical, such as in mobile devices and IoT.

Combining specialized low-power components with higher power components in a 3D stack allows for optimized power usage, leading to increased energy efficiency in the overall system. Stacking memory chips alongside processing units or other specialized chips minimizes data transfer distance and reduces latency, thereby improving system bandwidth and overall efficiency.

Heterogeneous integration enables the creation of custom-designed solutions for specific applications by combining components tailored to meet the requirements of the device. This optimization increases functionality in the specific use case. With the ability to combine different technologies in a 3D stack, designers have increased flexibility to create products that are more specialized and tailored for specific applications. The combination of diverse functionalities in close proximity allows for a more optimized and efficient overall system performance. This leads to better performance, functionality, and energy efficiency in electronic devices.

Heterogeneous integration in 3D chip stacking has significantly expanded the potential for combining different types of chips and technologies, enabling more compact, powerful, and energy-efficient electronic devices tailored to specific applications and use cases.

Techniques for 3D Chip Stacking

Through-Silicon Via (TSV) TSVs are vertical interconnects that penetrate through the silicon substrate, connecting different layers. They provide electrical and thermal connections between the stacked chips. TSVs are vertical interconnections that pass through the silicon wafer, connecting different layers of chips. TSVs provide a pathway for data, power, and heat transfer between stacked layers, enhancing communication and thermal management.

Encapsulation and Packaging Techniques involves advanced encapsulation and packaging methods are employed to protect the 3D stacked structure from environmental factors and to ensure durability and reliability. Design and Simulation Tools involves advanced computer-aided design (CAD) and simulation tools are used for layout design, modelling, and analysis of the 3D structures to optimize performance, mitigate issues, and plan for effective implementation. Testing and Yield Enhancement techniques are developed for testing the functionality and reliability of the 3D stacked structure, as well as strategies to improve the yield and quality of the manufactured chips.

Die Stacking technique, individual dies are stacked on top of each other, and interconnects are established using wire bonding or flip-chip technology. Die-to-Wafer Bonding technique involves bonding individual dies (semiconductor chips) onto a single wafer to form a stacked configuration. It helps in aligning and bonding multiple chips efficiently, often using techniques like micro-bumping or direct bonding.

Fan-Out Wafer-Level Packaging (FOWLP) technique involves redistributing the I/O connections from the chip to the package substrate, allowing for compact stacking. Wafer-to-Wafer Bonding technique, whole wafers are bonded together, allowing for the creation of multiple 3D stacked structures simultaneously. Advanced alignment and bonding technologies are employed to ensure precision and uniformity. Thermal Management Solutions is an innovative thermal management techniques, such as incorporating heat spreaders, advanced thermal interface materials, and cooling solutions within the stacked structure, are employed to manage and dissipate heat effectively.

Thin Die Handling and Thinning Techniques is the thinning of individual dies (thin-wafer handling) to reduce thickness allows for stacking multiple chips efficiently, ensuring manageable overall thickness in the 3D structure. Techniques like backside thinning or grinding are used for this purpose. Heterogeneous Integration Methods involves techniques are developed to integrate different types of chips, such as processors, memory, sensors, and RF components, ensuring effective coexistence and operation within the 3D structure. These techniques collectively contribute to the successful implementation of 3D chip stacking, ensuring efficient vertical integration of chips and enabling the creation of more powerful, compact, and energy-efficient semiconductor devices.

Applications of 3D Chip Stacking

Micro-Bumping and Micro-Interconnects is where small-scale connections are used to establish electrical connections between the stacked chips. Precise and high-density micro-bumping techniques ensure proper connectivity in 3D chip stacking. 3D stacking enhances data processing capabilities in supercomputers and data centres by improving speed and reducing power consumption. Space-constrained mobile devices benefit from the space-saving advantages of 3D stacking, allowing for more components in a smaller footprint. Stacked chips enable IoT devices to have multiple functionalities in a compact design, improving efficiency and connectivity. 3D stacking is used to increase memory capacity and bandwidth in applications like graphics cards and data storage systems. Embedded systems benefit from the improved performance and power efficiency offered by 3D chip stacking. In conclusion, 3D chip stacking is a transformative technology that addresses the challenges posed by Miniaturisation and increased functionality in semiconductor devices. Its benefits include improved performance, power efficiency, and space utilization, making it a promising solution for a wide range of applications across various industries.

The Future

The future of semiconductor technology holds tremendous promise and potential for groundbreaking advancements. As traditional scaling approaches reach physical limits, researchers are exploring new techniques such as nanotechnology, 3D stacking, and alternative materials to continue improving performance and energy efficiency beyond the limitations of Moore's Law. This might involve novel architectures and computing paradigms.

Quantum computing, utilizing quantum bits (qubits), offers the potential for unprecedented computational power by solving complex problems exponentially faster than classical computers. However, practical challenges in maintaining qubits' coherence and scalability need to be addressed for its widespread adoption. Specialized hardware optimized for artificial intelligence and machine learning applications, like neuromorphic computing and analogue computing, will continue to advance, providing faster and more energy-efficient solutions for AI tasks.

 Advancements in semiconductor technologies will improve the efficiency of power electronics, enabling better energy conversion in various applications, from electric vehicles to renewable energy systems. Smaller, more sensitive, and energy-efficient sensors will drive the expansion of IoT devices, creating smarter and more interconnected systems for both consumer and industrial use. Semiconductor technology will further revolutionize healthcare with miniaturized and more accurate diagnostic tools, wearable health monitors, and implantable devices for personalized medicine and continuous health monitoring.

Development of faster, denser, and more reliable memory and storage solutions such as MRAM (Magnetoresistive RAM) and RRAM (Resistive RAM) will offer significant improvements in data storage and retrieval.

Integrating photonics with traditional electronics could lead to faster data transfer and reduced energy consumption in data centres and high-performance computing. Advancements in semiconductor technology will likely focus on enhancing security features within hardware to counter evolving cybersecurity threats, focusing on secure encryption, authentication, and tamper-resistant devices. The future of semiconductor technology is driven by innovation, addressing challenges, and exploring new frontiers to enable more powerful, efficient, and versatile applications across various industries.

www.ingramcontent.com/pod-product-compliance
Lightning Source LLC
La Vergne TN
LVHW081531050326
832903LV00025B/1735